# The Rosary in Latin and English

## SECOND EDITION

# The Rosary in Latin and English

**SECOND EDITION**

*Edited by*
Geoffrey W.M.P. Lopes da Silva

**DOMINA NOSTRA PUBLISHING**
Monterey, California, USA

Published in 2021 by
Domina Nostra Publishing
P.O. Box 1464, Monterey, CA. 93942-1464 USA
Email: info@DominaNostraPublishing.com
Website: www.DominaNostraPublishing.com

Copyright © 2021 Domina Nostra Publishing

Printed and bound in the United States of America.
All rights reserved.

Cover: *Madonna del Rosario* by Simone Cantarini (1612-1648).

For a complete list of sources, see the bibliography on page 101.

Although the editor and publisher have made every effort to ensure the accuracy and completeness of information contained in this book, we assume no responsibility for errors, inaccuracies, omissions, or any inconsistency herein. Any slights of people, places, or organizations are unintentional, and will be corrected in the next edition.

Second edition and first printing, 2021.

ISBN: 978-0-9741900-7-5

Library of Congress Control Number: 2020915803

This book is most humbly dedicated
to the Most Blessed Virgin Mary of Fátima,
Queen of the Most Holy Rosary.

# Contents

Preface — 9
*Præfatio*

Introduction — 11
*Prœmium*

The Recitation of the Marian Rosary — 15
*Rosarii Marialis recitatio*

The Prayers of the Rosary — 21
*Orationes Rosarii*

The Mysteries of the Rosary — 41
*Mysteria Rosarii*

Appendices

I. Various Prayers — 93
   *Orationes variæ*

II. The Rosary Novena — 96
    *Novendiales*

III. Indulgences — 98
     *Indulgentiæ*

Bibliography — 101
*Bibliographia*

*Index generalis* — 103

# Preface
## *Præfatio*

*The Rosary in Latin and English* was the very first book published by Domina Nostra Publishing in October of 2003.

The decision to publish the prayers of the Rosary in Latin and English had come almost naturally, and in the end seemed providential, considering that from its very inception, this publishing house was placed under the patronage of *Domina Nostra*—Our Lady.

Nearly 20 years have passed and the time has come to publish this revised edition of *The Rosary in Latin and English*. In order to better aid in meditation, traditional images for each mystery, as well as expanded readings from Sacred Scripture, are now included.

> Let us, therefore, ever honour the most holy Mother of God by the devotion very dear to her. May she who so many times has answered the prayers of Christ's faithful in the recitation of the Rosary, who brought their earthly enemies to destruction and defeat, grant victory over the powers of hell to us also.[1]

Geoffrey W.M.P. Lopes da Silva
Publisher and Executive Editor

---

[1] « *Sanctissimam ergo Dei Genitricem cultu hoc eidem gratissimo iugiter veneremur ut quæ toties Christi fidelibus, Rosarii precibus exorata, terrenos hostes profligare dedit ac perdere, infernos pariter superare concedat* » (*Breviarium Romanum*, editio typica 1961, die 7 octobris, B. Mariæ Virg. a Rosario, ad Matutinum).

## Introduction
### *Præmium*

The word rosary, from the Latin *rosarium* (meaning "crown" or "garland of roses"), refers to "a string of beads consisting of five sets (decades) each of ten small and one larger bead (a crucifix with two large and three small beads is ordinarily added)".

The word rosary also refers to "the prayers said on these beads. Each decade is associated with a mystery of the faith... The tradition that the rosary was revealed by our Lady to Saint Dominic is unproven; but the devotion has been particularly associated with his order for over 400 years".[1]

The Rosary "is one of the most excellent prayers to the Mother of God. Thus, 'the Roman Pontiffs have repeatedly exhorted the faithful to the frequent recitation of this biblically inspired prayer which is centred on contemplation of the salvific events of Christ's life, and their close association with His Virgin Mother. The value and efficacy of this prayer have often been attested by saintly Bishops and those advanced in holiness of life'".[2]

This prayer book has been designed for those who wish to pray the Rosary in either English or Latin, which remains the official language of the Church. As Pope Benedict XVI said when presenting the *Compendium of the Catechism of the Catholic Church*,

---

[1] DONALD ATTWATER, *A Catholic Dictionary* (1958), p. 438.
[2] CONGREGATION FOR DIVINE WORSHIP AND THE DISCIPLINE OF THE SACRAMENTS, *Directory on Popular Piety and the Liturgy: Principles and Guidelines* (December 2001), n. 197; cf. CONGREGATION FOR DIVINE WORSHIP, *Circular Letter Guidelines and proposals for the celebration of the Marian Year*, 62.

learning the prayers of the Rosary in Latin "will make it easier for the Christian faithful who speak different languages to pray together, especially when they meet for special circumstances".

> As I said in 1997, on the occasion of the presentation to my Venerable Predecessor of the Typical Edition in Latin of the *Catechism of the Catholic Church*: "Precisely in the multiplicity of languages and cultures, Latin, for so many centuries the vehicle and instrument of Christian culture, not only guarantees continuity with our roots but continues to be as relevant as ever for strengthening the bonds of unity of the faith in the communion of the Church".[1]

Each mystery of the Rosary in this volume is accompanied by a picture which, according to Saint John Paul II, can help to "focus our attention".

> In the Church's traditional spirituality, the veneration of icons and the many devotions appealing to the senses [...] make use of visual and imaginative elements (the *compositio loci*), judged to be of great help in concentrating the mind on the particular mystery. This is a methodology, moreover, which corresponds to the inner logic of the Incarnation: in Jesus, God wanted to take on human features. It is through His bodily reality that we are led into contact with the mystery of His divinity.[2]

---

[1] BENEDICT XVI, *Address: Presentation of the Compendium of the Catechism of the Catholic Church* (28 June 2005), n. 8.
[2] « Spiritalem intra doctrinam, quæ in Ecclesia enucleata est, simul veneratio imaginum simul plures pietatis formæ sensibilibus elementis copiosæ [...] ad partem quandam visivam et prospectivam (quæ compositio loci nuncupatur), decurrunt quippe quam admodum utilem esse censeant ad fovendam animi intentionem in mysterium ipsum. Est via præterea quæ *structuræ Incarnationis logicæ ipsi convenit:* in Iesu enim decrevit Deus hominis induere

Each picture is accompanied by the words of the Angelic Salutation (Hail Mary) that contain the appropriate text for those wishing to make use of one of Saint Louis Marie de Montfort's optional methods for reciting the Rosary:

> Of celebrating the life, death, and heavenly glory of Jesus and Mary in the Holy Rosary and a method of restraining our imagination and lessening distractions. To do this a word or two is added to each Hail Mary of the decade reminding us of the mystery we are celebrating. This addition follows the name of Jesus in the middle of the Hail Mary.[1]

Each mystery is also accompanied by a brief reading from Sacred Scripture in order to, as Saint John Paul II said, "supply a Biblical foundation and greater depth to our meditation".

> No other words can ever match the efficacy of the inspired word. As we listen, we are certain that this is the word of God, spoken for today and spoken 'for me'. If received in this way, the word of God can become part of the Rosary's methodology of repetition without giving rise to the ennui derived from the simple recollection of something already well known. It is not a matter of recalling information but of allowing God to speak.[2]

---

formas. Per corpoream eius veritatem illuc adducimur ut mysterium ipsius divinum contingamus » (SANCTUS IOANNES PAULUS II, Epistola Apostolica *Rosarium Virginis Mariæ* (16 Octobris 2002), n. 29: *Acta Apostolicæ Sedis* 95 [2003], 26).

[1] SAINT LOUIS MARIE DE MONFORT, Methods for Saying the Rosary: *God Alone: The Collected Writings of St. Louis Marie de Monfort* (Montfort Publications, 1987), p. 237.

[2] « Numquam enim consequuntur aliena verba sermonis inspirati propriam efficacitatem. Hic enim audiatur oportet, cum certo constet Verbum esse Dei in hodiernum tempus ac "pro me" prolatum. Sic acceptus sermo divinus in ipsam repetitionis Rosarii ingreditur viam neque tædium gignit quod simplici appellatione ad

In his Apostolic Letter *Rosarium Virginis Mariæ*, Pope Saint John Paul II spoke about the importance of silence when praying the Rosary:

> *Listening and meditation are nourished by silence.* After the announcement of the mystery and the proclamation of the word, it is fitting to pause and focus one's attention for a suitable period of time on the mystery concerned, before moving into vocal prayer. A discovery of the importance of silence is one of the secrets of practicing contemplation and meditation. One drawback of a society dominated by technology and the mass media is the fact that silence becomes increasingly difficult to achieve. Just as moments of silence are recommended in the Liturgy, so too in the recitation of the Rosary it is fitting to pause briefly after listening to the word of God, while the mind focuses on the content of a particular mystery.[1]

---

rerum notitias iam diu comparatas gigneretur. Nullo modo: non interest in memoriam revocare rei cuiusdam cognitionem, verum *Deum "loqui" sinere* » (SANCTUS IOANNES PAULUS II, Epistola Apostolica *Rosarium Virginis Mariæ* (16 Octobris 2002), n. 30: *Acta Apostolicæ Sedis* 95 [2003], 27).

[1] « *Silentio aluntur auditio ac meditatio.* Consentaneum est ut mysterio nuntiato Verboque proclamato aliquamdiu consistatur ut mens in mysterium propositum dirigatur, priusquam vocalis precatio incipiat. Silentii utilitas iterum detecta unum est ex secretis ad contemplationem et meditationem exercitandam. Intra societatis limites, quæ technologia funditus permeatur instrumentisque universalis communicationis, patet etiam difficilius usque evadere ipsum silentium. Sicut enim in Liturgia silentii commendantur intervalla, ita etiam in Rosarii recitatione brevior mora opportuna est post Verbum Dei auditum, dum nempe in certi cuiusdam mysterii doctrina animus immoratur » (SANCTUS IOANNES PAULUS II, Epistola Apostolica *Rosarium Virginis Mariæ* (16 Octobris 2002), n. 31: *Acta Apostolicæ Sedis* 95 [2003], 27).

# The Recitation of the Marian Rosary
## *Rosarii Marialis recitatio*

In general, "the method of saying the Rosary, in public or private, is to recite an Our Father (large bead), ten Hail Marys (small beads), and Glory be to the Father (large bead), while meditating on the appropriate mystery; the essence of the devotion consists in a loving and intelligent meditation and not a mechanical repetition of the prayers. The beads are simply a device for keeping count".[1]

1. A **hymn**, such as *O Queen of the Holy Rosary* (page 94), may be sung, particularly in communal recitation. Another appropriate hymn may be selected, such as a Marian hymn or a hymn in keeping with the liturgical season, feast day, etc. A **Prayer before the Rosary** may also be said (page 95ff.).

2. The recitation of the Marian Rosary officially begins with the **Sign of the Cross** (p. 23). The **Apostles' Creed** (p. 23) and the **Lord's Prayer** or **Our Father** (p. 25) may then follow.

   The **Angelic Salutation** or **Hail Mary** (p. 25) may then said three times, traditionally for the three theological virtues of faith, hope, and charity. This is then followed by the **Minor Doxology** or **Glory to the Father** (p. 25).

   > At present, in different parts of the Church, there are many ways to introduce the Rosary. In some places, it is customary to begin with the opening words of Psalm 70: "O God, come to my assistance; O Lord, make haste to help me", as if to nourish in those who are

---
[1] Donald Attwater, *A Catholic Dictionary* (1958), p. 438.

praying a humble awareness of their own insufficiency. In other places, the Rosary begins with the recitation of the Creed, as if to make the profession of faith the basis of the contemplative journey about to be undertaken. These and similar customs, to the extent that they prepare the mind for contemplation, are all equally legitimate.[1]

3. The first mystery (*mystérium*) is then announced.

The Rosary can be recited in full every day, and there are those who most laudably do so. In this way it fills with prayer the days of many a contemplative, or keeps company with the sick and the elderly who have abundant time at their disposal. Yet it is clear—and this applies all the more if the new series of *mysteria lucis* is included—that many people will not be able to recite more than a part of the Rosary, according to a certain weekly pattern...[2]

---

[1] « In vigente Ecclesiæ usu multiplices exstant modi Rosarium inducendi secundum diversa adiuncta ecclesialia. Quibusdam locis Rosarium incipi solet invocatione Psalmi 69: "Deus, in adiutorium meum intende; Domine, ad adiuvandum me festina", ut in orante quasi humilis conscientia propriæ indigentiæ nutriatur; alibi contra, principium fit per symbolum apostolicum Credo tamquam si fidei professio iaciatur uti viæ contemplativæ fundamentum quæ suscipitur. Hi et similes modi quatenus mentem recte ad contemplationem conformant sunt pariter liciti » (SANCTUS IOANNES PAULUS II, Epistola Apostolica *Rosarium Virginis Mariæ* (16 Octobris 2002), n. 37: *Acta Apostolicæ Sedis* 95 [2003], 31).

[2] « Totum cotidie recitari licet Rosarium nec desunt qui id faciant. Sic enim precatione replet dies tot contemplativorum hominum atque infirmos et senes commitatur quibus satis est temporis. Patet tamen—et magis hoc valet si novus circuitus additur mysteriorum lucis—plures non persolvere posse nisi partem tantum secundum certum quendam hebdomadis ordinem... » (SANCTUS IOANNES PAULUS II, Epistola Apostolica *Rosarium Virginis Mariæ* (16 Octobris 2002), n. 38: *Acta Apostolicæ Sedis* 95 [2003], 31).

## Traditional Distribution

Joyful Mysteries:     Monday and Thursday
Sorrowful Mysteries:   Tuesday and Friday
Glorious Mysteries:    Wednesday, Saturday, and Sunday

## Contemporary Distribution

Joyful Mysteries:     Monday and Saturday
Luminous Mysteries:   Thursday
Sorrowful Mysteries:   Tuesday and Friday
Glorious Mysteries:    Wednesday and Sunday

> This indication is not intended to limit a rightful freedom in personal and community prayer, where account needs to be taken of spiritual and pastoral needs and of the occurrence of particular liturgical celebrations which might call for suitable adaptations. What is really important is that the Rosary should always be seen and experienced as a path of contemplation. In the Rosary, in a way similar to what takes place in the Liturgy, the Christian week, centred on Sunday, the day of Resurrection, becomes a journey through the mysteries of the life of Christ, and He is revealed in the lives of His disciples as the Lord of time and of history.[1]

---

[1] « Non vult tamen hoc consilium libertatem consentaneam in singulorum atque communitatum meditatione circumscribere, videlicet secundum spiritales pastoralesque necessitates at in primis liturgicas celebrationes quæ aptationes suadere possunt opportuniores. Id tamen quod summi interest hoc est, ut semper magis concipiatur et vivatur Rosarium tamquam contemplationis via. Per illam enim, perficiens ea quæ in Liturgia sacra aguntur, christianorum hebdomada ad diem Dominicum nempe Resurrectionis adhærens transit in cursum quendam per vitæ Christi mysteria, atque Ille sic se in vita suorum discipulorum affirmat veluti temporis historiæque Dominum » (SANCTUS IOANNES PAULUS II, Epistola Apostolica *Rosarium Virginis Mariæ* (16 Octobris 2002), n. 38: *Acta Apostolicæ Sedis* 95 [2003], 32).

*The Rosary in Latin and English*

4. The **Lord's Prayer** (page 25) is said once, followed by the **Angelic Salutation** (page 25) ten times while meditating on the announced mystery.

5. The **Minor Doxology** or **Glory to the Father** (page 25) is said to conclude the decade. On the last three days of Holy Week, this may be replaced by the antiphon from Saint Paul's letter to the Philippians (2:8-9) (page 25 and 27).

6. The **Fatima Prayer** (page 27) may then be said.

7. When praying the Rosary for the repose of the souls of the faithful departed, the **Brief Responsory for the Dead** (page 27) may be added after each decade.

8. After the five (or more) decades are completed, either a **Marian Antiphon** (page 29) or the **Litany of Loreto** (page 31) is said.

9. The **Prayer Concluding the Rosary** (page 35) is then said, which comes from the 1962 edition of the *Missale Romanum* (Roman Missal).

10. Prayers for the intentions of the Pope, the local bishop, and for the repose of the souls of the Faithful Departed may then be said (p. 35ff.).

> The Rosary is then ended with a prayer for the intentions of the Pope, as if to expand the vision of the one praying to embrace all the needs of the Church. It is precisely in order to encourage this ecclesial dimension of the Rosary that the Church has seen fit to grant

indulgences to those who recite it with the required dispositions.[1]

11. The recitation of the Rosary is then concluded with a **Blessing** (p. 37). This may take the form of a simple Sign of the Cross. When the Rosary is led by a priest or deacon in communal recitation, it would be appropriate for him to conclude with a liturgical blessing and dismissal.

12. The symbols ℣. for **verse** (or **versicle**) and ℟. for **response** denotes how the prayers may be said when the Rosary is recited in common.

---

[1] « Terminatur deinde prece secundum Pontificis mentem ut precantis oculi in latissimum prospectum aperiantur Ecclesiæ totius necessitatum. Et ut hæc ecclesialis Rosarii ratio proveheretur, voluit illud Ecclesia sanctis indulgentiis locupletare pro debito modo recitantibus » (SANCTUS IOANNES PAULUS II, Epistola Apostolica *Rosarium Virginis Mariæ* (16 Octobris 2002), n. 37: *Acta Apostolicæ Sedis* 95 [2003], 31).

# The Prayers of the Rosary
## *Orationes Rosarii*

*"Never will a soul
faithful to the daily recitation of the Rosary
be guilty of formal heresy
or be deceived by the devil.
These words I am willing to endorse
with my own blood".*

SAINT LOUIS DE MONTFORT
1673-1716

## Signum crucis

℣. In nómine Patris, ✠ et Fílii,
et Spíritus Sancti. ℟. Amen.

Vel:

℣. Deus, ✠ in adiutórium meum inténde.
℟. Dómine, ad adiuvándum me festína.[1]

℣. Glória Patri, et Fílio,
et Spirítui Sancto.
℟. Sicut erat in princípio, et nunc et semper,
et in sǽcula sæculórum. Amen.

## Symbolum Apostolorum

℣. Credo in Deum,
Patrem omnipoténtem,
Creatórem cæli et terræ,
et in Iesum Christum,
Fílium eius únicum, Dóminum nostrum,
*qui concéptus est de Spíritu Sancto,
natus ex María Vírgine,*[2]
passus sub Póntio Piláto,
crucifíxus, mórtuus, et sepúltus,
descéndit ad ínferos,
tértia die resurréxit a mórtuis,
ascéndit ad cælos,
sedet ad déxteram Dei
Patris omnipoténtis,
inde ventúrus est iudicáre
vivos et mórtuos.

℟. Credo in Spíritum Sanctum,
sanctam Ecclésiam cathólicam,
sanctórum communiónem,
remissiónem peccatórum,
carnis resurrectiónem,
vitam ætérnam. Amen.

---

[1] *Psalmus* 69 (70), 2.
[2] Omnes se inclinant.

*The Prayers of the Rosary (Orationes Rosarii)*

## THE SIGN OF THE CROSS

V̆. In the name of the Father, ✠ and of the Son,
and of the Holy Spirit. R̆. Amen.

Or:

V̆. O God, ✠ come to my assistance.
R̆. O Lord, make haste to help me.[1]

V̆. Glory to the Father, and to the Son,
and to the Holy Spirit.
R̆. As it was in the beginning, is now,
and will be for ever. Amen.

## THE APOSTLES' CREED

V̆. I BELIEVE IN GOD,
the Father almighty,
Creator of heaven and earth,
and in Jesus Christ,
His only Son, our Lord,
*who was conceived by the Holy Spirit,*
*born of the Virgin Mary,*[2]
suffered under Pontius Pilate,
was crucified, died and was buried;
He descended into hell;
on the third day He rose again from the dead;
He ascended into heaven,
and is seated at the right hand of God
the Father almighty;
from there He will come to judge
the living and the dead.

R̆. I believe in the Holy Spirit,
the holy catholic Church,
the communion of saint,
the forgiveness of sins,
the resurrection of the body,
and life everasting. Amen.

---

[1] *Psalm* 69 (70):2.
[2] All bow.

## Oratio dominica[1]

℣. Pater noster, qui es in cælis:
sanctificétur nomen tuum;
advéniat regnum tuum;
fiat volúntas tua,
sicut in cælo, et in terra.

℟. Panem nostrum cotidiánum da nobis hódie;
et dimítte nobis débita nostra,
sicut et nos dimíttimus debitóribus nostris;
et ne nos indúcas in tentatiónem;
sed líbera nos a malo. Amen.

## Salutatio angelica[2]

℣. Ave, María, grátia plena,
Dóminus tecum.
Benedícta tu in muliéribus,
et benedíctus fructus ventris tui, Iesus.

℟. Sancta María, mater Dei,
ora pro nobis peccatóribus,
nunc et in hora mortis nostræ. Amen.

## Doxologia minor

℣. Glória Patri, et Fílio,
et Spirítui Sancto.

℟. Sicut erat in princípio, et nunc et semper,
et in sǽcula sæculórum. Amen.

Vel:

### Feria Quinta in Cena Domini

℣. Christus factus est pro nobis.

℟. Oboédiens usque ad mortem.

---

[1] *Matthæum* 6, 9-13; cf. *Lucam* 11, 2-4.
[2] Cf. *Lucam* 1, 28 et 1, 42.

*The Prayers of the Rosary (Orationes Rosarii)*

## THE LORD'S PRAYER[1]

℣. OUR FATHER, who art in heaven,
hallowed be thy name;
thy kingdom come,
thy will be done
on earth as it is in heaven.

℟. Give us this day our daily bread,
and forgive us our trespasses,
as we forgive those who trespass against us;
and lead us not into temptation,
but deliver us from evil. Amen.

## THE ANGELIC SALUTATION[2]

℣. HAIL, MARY, full of grace,
the Lord is with you;
blessed are you among women,
and blessed is the fruit of your womb, Jesus.

℟. Holy Mary, Mother of God,
pray for us sinners
now and at the hour of our death. Amen.

## THE MINOR DOXOLOGY

℣. GLORY BE TO THE FATHER, and to the Son,
and to the Holy Spirit.

℟. As it was in the beginning, is now,
and ever shall be, world without end. Amen.

Or:

### Holy Thursday of the Lord's Supper

℣. Christ became obedient for us.

℟. Obedient unto death.

---

[1] *Matthew* 6:9-13; cf. *Luke* 11:2-4.
[2] Cf. *Luke* 1:28 and 1:42.

### Feria Sexta in Passione Domini

℣. Christus factus est pro nobis oboédiens usque ad mortem.

℟. Mortem autem crucis.

### Sabbato Sancto

℣. Christus factus est pro nobis oboédiens usque ad mortem,
mortem autem crucis.

℟. Propter quod et Deus exaltávit illum:
et dedit illi nomen,
quod est super omne nomen.[1]

Ad libitum:

## Oratio Fátima (Oratio decadis)

℣. O mi Iesu,

℟. dimítte nobis débita nostra,
líbera nos ab igne inférni,
conduc in cælum ómnes ánimas, præsértim illas,
quæ máxime índigent (misericórdia tua).

## Responsorium breve pro defunctis

℣. Réquiem ætérnam dona ei (eis), Dómine.

℟. Et lux perpétua lúceat ei (eis).

℣. Requiéscat (Requiéscant) in pace.

℟. Amen.

℣. Anima eius,
et ánimæ ómnium fidélium defunctórum
per misericórdiam Dei requiéscant in pace.

℟. Amen.

---
[1] Cf. *Philippenses* 2, 8-9.

*The Prayers of the Rosary (Orationes Rosarii)*

### Good Friday of the Passion of the Lord

V̆. Christ became obedient for us
 unto death.

R̆. Even to the death of the cross.

### Holy Saturday

V̆. Christ became obedient for us
 unto death,
 even to the death of the cross.

R̆. For which cause, God also has exalted Him
 and has given Him a name
 which is above all names.[1]

Optional:

### THE FÁTIMA PRAYER (DECADE PRAYER)

V̆. O MY JESUS,

R̆. forgive us our sins,
 save us from the fires of hell,
 lead all souls to heaven,
 especially those most in need (of Your mercy).

### BRIEF RESPONSORY FOR THE DEAD

V̆. ETERNAL REST grant unto him/her (them), O Lord.

R̆. And let perpetual light shine upon him/her (them).

V̆. May he / she (they) rest in peace.

R̆. Amen.

V̆. May his / her soul,
 and the souls of all the faithful departed,
 through the mercy of God rest in peace.

R̆. Amen.

---
[1] Cf. *Philippians* 2:8-9.

## Antiphona Mariana

In fine precationis laudabiliter additur Antiphona mariana (Salve, Regina), ut infra, vel **Litaniæ Laurentanæ**, p. 30.

Salve, Regína, mater misericórdiæ;
vita, dulcédo et spes nostra, salve.
Ad te clamámus éxsules fílii Hevæ.
Ad te suspirámus geméntes et flentes
in hac lacrimárum valle.
Eia ergo, advocáta nostra,
illos tuos misericórdes óculos ad nos convérte.
Et Iesum, benedíctum fructum ventris tui,
nobis post hoc exsílium osténde.
O clemens, o pia, o dulcis Virgo María.

Tempore Adventus et Nativitates et post mysteria gaudiosa recitata dici vel cani potest:

Alma Redemptóris Mater,
quæ pérvia cæli porta manes,
et stella maris, succúrre cadénti,
súrgere qui curat, pópulo:
tu quæ genuísti, natúra miránte,
tuum sanctum Genitórem,
Virgo prius ac postérius,
Gabriélis ab ore sumens illud Ave,
peccatórum miserére.

Tempore paschali et post mysteria gloriosa recitata dici vel cani potest antiphona:

Regína cæli lætáre, allelúia.
Quia quem meruísti portáre, allelúia.
Resurréxit, sicut dixit, allelúia.
Ora pro nobis Deum, allelúia.

*The Prayers of the Rosary (Orationes Rosarii)*

## MARIAN ANTIPHON

At the end of the prayer is laudably added the Marian Antiphon (Hail, Holy Queen), as below, or the **Litany of Loreto**, p. 31.

HAIL, HOLY QUEEN, mother of mercy,
our life, our sweetness, and our hope.
To thee do we cry, poor banished children of Eve.
To thee do we send up our sighs,
mourning and weeping in this vale of tears.
Turn then, most gracious advocate,
thine eyes of mercy toward us,
and after this our exile
show unto us the blessed fruit of thy womb, Jesus.
O clement, O loving, O sweet Virgin Mary.

During Advent, Christmas Time, and after the Joyful Mysteries are recited, the following antiphon may be said or sung:

MOTHER BENIGN OF OUR REDEEMING LORD,
Star of the sea and portal of the skies,
Unto thy fallen people help afford —
Fallen, but striving still anew to rise.
Thou who didst once,
while wondering worlds adored,
Bear thy Creator, Virgin then as now,
O by thy holy joy at Gabriel's word,
Pity the sinners who before thee bow.

During Easter Time and after the Glorious Mysteries are recited, the following antiphon may be said or sung:

QUEEN OF HEAVEN, rejoice, alleluia,
for He whom you were worthy to bear, alleluia,
has risen as He said, alleluia.
Pray for us to God, alleluia.

## Litaniæ lauretanæ Beatæ Mariæ virginis

Kýrie eléison. ℟. Kýrie eléison.
Christe eléison. ℟. Christe eléison.
Kýrie eléison. ℟. Kýrie eléison.

Christe, audi nos.
℟. Christe, exáudi nos.

Pater de cælis, Deus. ℟. Miserére nobis.
Fili Redémptor mundi, Deus. ℟.
Spíritus Sancte, Deus. ℟.
Sancta Trínitas, unus Deus. ℟.

Sancta María. ℟. Ora pro nobis.
Sancta Dei Génitrix. ℟.
Sancta Virgo Vírginum. ℟.

Mater Christi. ℟.
Mater Ecclésiæ. ℟.
Mater misericórdiæ. ℟.
Mater divínæ grátiæ. ℟.
Mater spei. ℟.
Mater puríssima. ℟.
Mater castíssima. ℟.
Mater inynoláta. ℟.
Mater intemeráta. ℟.
Mater immaculáta. ℟.
Mater amábilis. ℟.
Mater admirábilis. ℟.
Mater boni consílii. ℟.
Mater Creatóris. ℟.
Mater Salvatóris. ℟.

Virgo prudentíssima. ℟.
Virgo veneránda. ℟.
Virgo prædicánda. ℟.
Virgo potens. ℟.
Virgo clemens. ℟.
Virgo fidélis. ℟.

## LITANY OF LORETO OF THE BLESSED VIRGIN MARY

Lord, have mercy. ℟. Lord, have mercy.
Christ, have mercy. ℟. Christ, have mercy.
Lord, have mercy. ℟. Lord, have mercy.

Christ, hear us.
℟. Christ, graciously hear us.

God, the Father of heaven. ℟. Have mercy on us.
God the Son, Redeemer of the world. ℟.
God the Holy Spirit. ℟.
Holy Trinity, one God. ℟.

Holy Mary. ℟. Pray for us.
Holy Mother of God. ℟.
Holy Virgin of virgins. ℟.

Mother of Christ. ℟.
Mother of the Church. ℟.
Mother of mercy. ℟.
Mother of divine grace. ℟.
Mother of hope. ℟.
Mother most pure. ℟.
Mother most chaste. ℟.
Mother inviolate. ℟.
Mother undefiled. ℟.
Mother immaculate. ℟.
Mother most amiable. ℟.
Mother most admirable. ℟.
Mother of good counsel. ℟.
Mother of our Creator. ℟.
Mother of our Saviour. ℟.

Virgin most prudent. ℟.
Virgin most venerable. ℟.
Virgin most renowned. ℟.
Virgin most powerful. ℟.
Virgin most merciful. ℟.
Virgin most faithful. ℟.

Spéculum iustítiæ. ℟. Ora pro nobis.
Sedes sapiéntiæ. ℟.
Causa nostræ lætítiæ. ℟.
Vas spirituále. ℟.
Vas honorábile. ℟.
Vas insígne devotiónis. ℟.
Rosa mýstica. ℟.
Turris davídica. ℟.
Turris ebúrnea. ℟.
Domus áurea. ℟.
Foéderis arca. ℟.
Iánua cæli. ℟.
Stella matutína. ℟.
Salus infirmórum. ℟.
Refúgium peccatórum. ℟.
Solácium migrantium. ℟.
Consolátrix afflictórum. ℟.
Auxílium Christianórum. ℟.

Regína Angelórum. ℟.
Regína Patriarchárum. ℟.
Regína Prophetárum. ℟.
Regína Apostolórum. ℟.
Regína Mártyrum. ℟.
Regína Confessórum. ℟.
Regína Vírginum. ℟.
Regína Sanctórum ómnium. ℟.
Regína sine labe origináli concépta. ℟.
Regína in cælum assúmpta. ℟.
Regína sacratíssimi Rosárii. ℟.
Regina familiarum. ℟.
Regína pacis. ℟.

Agnus Dei, qui tollis peccáta mundi.
℟. Parce nobis, Dómine.

Agnus Dei, qui tollis peccáta mundi.
℟. Exáudi nos, Dómine.

Agnus Dei, qui tollis peccáta mundi.
℟. Miserére nobis.

*The Prayers of the Rosary (Orationes Rosarii)*

Mirror of justice. ℟. Pray for us.
Seat of wisdom. ℟.
Cause of our joy. ℟.
Spiritual vessel. ℟.
Vessel of honour. ℟.
Singular vessel of devotion. ℟.
Mystical rose. ℟.
Tower of David. ℟.
Tower of ivory. ℟.
House of gold. ℟.
Ark of the covenant. ℟.
Gate of heaven. ℟.
Morning star. ℟.
Health of the sick. ℟.
Refuge of sinners. ℟.
Comfort of migrants. ℟.
Comforter of the afflicted. ℟.
Help of Christians. ℟.

Queen of angels. ℟.
Queen of patriarchs. ℟.
Queen of prophets. ℟.
Queen of apostles. ℟.
Queen of martyrs. ℟.
Queen of confessors. ℟.
Queen of virgins. ℟.
Queen of all saints. ℟.
Queen conceived without original sin. ℟.
Queen assumed into heaven. ℟.
Queen of the most holy Rosary. ℟.
Queen of the family. ℟.
Queen of peace. ℟.

Lamb of God, You take away the sins of the world.
℟. Spare us, O Lord.

Lamb of God, You take away the sins of the world.
℟. Graciously hear us, O Lord.

Lamb of God, You take away the sins of the world.
℟. Have mercy on us.

## ORATIO AD FINEM ROSARII DICENDA

℣. Ora pro nobis, Sancta Dei Génetrix.

    Vel: Ora pro nobis, Regina sacratíssimi Rosárii.

℟. Ut digni efficiámur
promissiónibus Christi.

Orémus.

Deus, cuius Unigénitus
per vitam, mortem et resurrectiónem suam
nobis salútis ætérnæ præmia comparávit:
concéde, quǽsumus;
ut, hæc mystéria sacratíssimo
beátæ Maríæ Vírginis Rosário recoléntes,
et imitémur quod cóntinent,
et quod promíttunt assequámur.
Per eúndem Christum Dóminum nostrum. ℟. Amen.

Ad libitum:

(Orémus) pro beatíssimo Papa nostro N.:

℣. Pater noster. ℟. Panem nostrum.

℣. Ave, María. ℟. Sancta María.

℣. Glória Patri. ℟. Sicut erat.

(Orémus) pro Antístite nostro N.

℣. Pater noster. ℟. Panem nostrum.

℣. Ave, María. ℟. Sancta María.

℣. Glória Patri. ℟. Sicut erat.

## Prayer Concluding the Rosary

℣. Pray for us, O holy Mother of God.

    Or: Pray for us, O Queen of the most holy Rosary.

℟. That we may be made worthy
of the promises of Christ.

Let us pray.

O God, Whose only-begotten Son,
by His Life, Death, and Resurrection,
has purchased for us the rewards of eternal life:
grant, we beseech You,
that, meditating upon these mysteries
of the most holy Rosary of the Blessed Virgin Mary,
we may imitate what they contain
and obtain what they promise.
Through the same Christ our Lord. ℟. Amen.

Optional:

(Let us pray) for our Most Holy Father, Pope N.:

℣. Our Father... ℟. Give us this day...

℣. Hail, Mary... ℟. Holy Mary...

℣. Glory be to the Father... ℟. As it was...

(Let us pray) for our bishop, N.:

℣. Our Father... ℟. Give us this day...

℣. Hail, Mary... ℟. Holy Mary...

℣. Glory be to the Father... ℟. As it was...

(Orémus) pro fidélibus defúnctis.

℣. Pater noster. ℟. Panem nostrum.

℣. Ave, María. ℟. Sancta María.

℣. Réquiem ætérnam dona eis, Dómine.

℟. Et lux perpétua lúceat eis.

℣. Requiéscant in pace.

℟. Amen.

## BENEDICTIO

Absente sacerdote vel diacono, et in recitatione a solo:

℣. Nos cum prole pia benedícat ✠
Virgo María. ℟. Amen.

Vel:

℣. Dóminus nos benedícat, ✠
et ab omni malo deféndat,
et ad vitam perdúcat ætérnam. ℟. Amen.

Si præest sacerdos vel diaconus, populum dimittit, dicens:

℣. Dóminus vobíscum.

℟. Et cum spíritu tuo.

℣. Benedícat vos omnípotens Deus, ✠
Pater, et Fílius, et Spíritus Sanctus.

℟. Amen.

Et, si fit dimissio, sequitur invitatio:

℣. Ite in pace. ℟. Deo grátias.

*The Prayers of the Rosary (Orationes Rosarii)*

(Let us pray) for the faithful departed:

℣. Our Father... ℟. Give us this day...

℣. Hail, Mary... ℟. Holy Mary...

℣. Eternal rest grant unto them, O Lord.

℟. And let perpetual light shine upon them.

℣. May they rest in peace.

℟. Amen.

## BLESSING

In the absence of a priest or deacon and in individual recitation:

℣. May the Virgin Mary with her loving Child ✠ bless us. ℟. Amen.

Or:

℣. May the Lord bless us, ✠
protect us from all evil
and bring us to everlasting life. ℟. Amen.

If a priest or deacon presides, he dismisses the people:

℣. The Lord be with you.

℟. And with your spirit.

℣. May almighty God bless you, ✠
the Father, and the Son, and the Holy Spirit.

℟. Amen.

Then he adds:

℣. Go in peace. ℟. Thanks be to God.

## Oratio ad S. Ioseph

Ad te beáte Ioseph,
in tribulatióne nostra confúgimus,
atque, imploráto Sponsæ tuæ sanctíssimæ auxílio,
patrocínium quoque tuum fidénter expóscimus.

Per eam, quǽsumus quæ te
cum immaculáta Vírgine Dei Genetríce coniúnxit,
caritátem, perque patérnum,
quo Púerum Iesum ampléxus es, amórem,
súpplices deprecámur,
ut ad hereditátem,
quam Iesus Christus acquisívit Sánguine suo,
benígnus respícias,
ac necessitátibus nostris tua virtúte et ope succúrras.

Tuére, o Custos providentíssime divínæ Famíliæ,
Iesu Christi sóbolem eléctam;
próhibe a nobis, amantíssime Pater,
omnem errórum ac corruptelárum luem;
propítius nobis, sospitátor noster fortíssime,
in hoc cum potestáte tenebrárum certámine
e cælo adésto;
et sicut olim Púerum Iesum
e summo eripuísti vitæ discrímine,
ita nunc Ecclésiam sanctam Dei
ab hostílibus insídiis
atque ab omni adversitáte defénde:
nosque síngulos perpétuo tege patrocínio,
ut ad tui exémplar et ope tua suffúlti,
sancte vívere, pie émori,
sempiternámque in cælis beatitúdinem
ássequi possímus. Amen.

*The Prayers of the Rosary (Orationes Rosarii)*

## PRAYER TO ST JOSEPH[1]

To you, O blessed Joseph,
we come in our trials,
and having asked the help of your most holy spouse,
we confidently ask your patronage also.

Through that sacred bond of charity which united you
to the Immaculate Virgin Mother of God
and through the fatherly love
with which you embraced the Child Jesus,
we humbly beg you
to look graciously upon the beloved inheritance
which Jesus Christ purchased by His blood,
and to aid us in our necessities
with your power and strength.

O most provident guardian of the Holy Family,
defend the chosen children of Jesus Christ.
Most beloved father,
dispel the evil of falsehood and sin.
Our most mighty protector,
graciously assist us from heaven in our struggle
with the powers of darkness.
And just as you once saved the Child Jesus
from mortal danger,
so now defend God's Holy Church
from the snares of her enemies
and from all adversity.
Shield each one of us by your constant protection,
so that, supported by your example and your help,
we may be able to live a virtuous life,
to die a holy death,
and to obtain eternal happiness in heaven. Amen.

---

[1] In some places, this prayer of Pope Leo XIII (1810-1903), 256th Bishop of Rome, is said after the recitation of the Holy Rosary during the months of March and October.

# The Mysteries of the Rosary
## *Mysteria Rosarii*

*"This prayer is a synthesis of our faith,
the support of our hope,
the explosion of our charity".*

SAINT PIO OF PIETRELCINA
1887-1968

# Mystéria gaudiósa

### in feria secunda et sabbato

Primus circulus, qui est « mysteriorum gaudiosorum », signatur revera lætitia ex Incarnationis eventu effulgente...

Significat igitur « gaudiosa » ponderare mysteria, nempe in ultimas intrare rationes significationemque christianæ lætitiæ intimam. Significat etiam oculos in veritatem concretam dirigere Incarnationis mysterii atque etiam in mysterii salvifici doloris prænuntiationem obscuriorem. Eo ducit nos Maria ut gaudii christiani secretum comprehendamus et reminiscamur christianum nomen in primis esse euangelion, « nuntium bonum », quod medium suum elementum immo ipsum suum magisterium in Christi persona, qui est Verbum caro factum, unicus orbis Salvator.

S. IOANNES PAULUS II

Epistula apostolica *Rosarium Virginis Mariæ*
(16 octobris 2002), n. 20:
*Acta Apostolicae Sedis* 95 (2003) 18-19

## The Joyful Mysteries

on Monday and Saturday[1]

The first five decades, the "joyful mysteries", are marked by the joy radiating from the event of the Incarnation...

To meditate upon the "joyful" mysteries, then, is to enter into the ultimate causes and the deepest meaning of Christian joy. It is to focus on the realism of the mystery of the Incarnation and on the obscure foreshadowing of the mystery of the saving Passion. Mary leads us to discover the secret of Christian joy, reminding us that Christianity is, first and foremost, euangelion, "good news", which has as its heart and its whole content the person of Jesus Christ, the Word made flesh, the one Saviour of the world.

St John Paul II

Apostolic Letter *Rosarium Virginis Mariæ*
(16 October 2002), n. 20

---

[1] For those who choose not to observe the Luminous Mysteries (*mystéria luminósa*), the Joyful Mysteries (*mystéria gaudiósa*) are said on Monday and Thursday. In some places, the Joyful Mysteries (*mystéria gaudiósa*) are said on the Sundays of Advent and daily during the Octave of Christmas (*Octava Nativitatis*).

Hail, Mary, full of grace, the Lord is with thee; blessed art thou amongst women, and blessed is the fruit of thy womb, Jesus, **Whom thou didst conceive**. Holy Mary, Mother of God, pray for us sinners now and at the hour of our death. Amen.

*Ave, María, grátia plena, Dóminus tecum. Benedícta tu in muliéribus, et benedíctus fructus ventris tui, Iesus,* **Quem, Virgo, concepísti**. *Sancta María, Mater Dei, ora pro nobis peccatóribus, nunc et in hora mortis nostræ. Amen.*

## The First Joyful Mystery
## The Annunciation

The angel Gabriel was sent from God to a city of Galilee named Nazareth, to a virgin betrothed to a man whose name was Joseph, of the house of David; and the virgin's name was Mary. And he came to her and said, "Hail, full of grace, the Lord is with you! [...]

"Do not be afraid, Mary, for you have found favor with God. And behold, you will conceive in your womb and bear a son, and you shall call his name Jesus. [...] The Holy Spirit will come upon you, and the power of the Most High will overshadow you; therefore the child to be born will be called holy, the Son of God". [...]

And Mary said, "Behold, I am the handmaid of the Lord; let it be to me according to your word".[1]

## Prímum mystérium gaudiósum
## Annuntiátio

Missus est ángelus Gábriel a Deo in civitátem Galilaéæ, cui nomen Názareth, ad vírginem desponsátam viro, cui nomen erat Ioseph de domo David, et nomen vírginis María. Et ingréssus ad eam dixit: « Ave, grátia plena, Dóminus tecum. [...]

Ne tímeas, María; invenísti enim grátiam apud Deum. Et ecce concípies in útero et páries fílium, et vocábis nomen eius Iesum. [...] Spíritus Sanctus supervéniet in te, et virtus Altíssimi obumbrábit tibi: ideóque et quod nascétur sanctum, vocábitur Fílius Dei ». [...]

Dixit autem María: « Ecce ancílla Dómini; fiat mihi secúndum verbum tuum ».[2]

---
[1] *Luke* 1:26-28. 30b-31. 35b. 38.
[2] *Lucam* 1, 26-28. 30b-31. 35b. 38.

Hail, Mary, full of grace, the Lord is with thee; blessed art thou amongst women, and blessed is the fruit of thy womb, Jesus, **Whom thou didst carry while visiting Elizabeth**. Holy Mary, Mother of God, pray for us sinners now and at the hour of our death. Amen.

*Ave, María, grátia plena, Dóminus tecum. Benedícta tu in muliéribus, et benedíctus fructus ventris tui, Iesus, **Quem visitándo Elísabeth portásti**. Sancta María, Mater Dei, ora pro nobis peccatóribus, nunc et in hora mortis nostræ. Amen.*

## The Second Joyful Mystery
## The Visitation

In those days Mary arose and went with haste into the hill country, to a city of Judah, and she entered the house of Zechariah and greeted Elizabeth. And when Elizabeth heard the greeting of Mary, the babe leaped in her womb; and Elizabeth was filled with the Holy Spirit and she exclaimed with a loud cry, "Blessed are you among women, and blessed is the fruit of your womb! And why is this granted me, that the mother of my Lord should come to me? For behold, when the voice of your greeting came to my ears, the babe in my womb leaped for joy. And blessed is she who believed that there would be a fulfilment of what was spoken to her from the Lord". [...]

And Mary remained with her about three months, and returned to her home.[1]

## Secúndum mystérium gaudiósum
## Visitátio

Exsúrgens María in diébus illis ábiit in montána cum festinatióne in civitátem Iudæ et intrávit in domum Zacharíæ et salutávit Elísabeth. Et factum est ut audívit salutatiónem Maríæ Elísabeth, exsultávit infans in útero eius, et repléta est Spíritu Sancto Elísabeth et exclamávit voce magna et dixit: « Benedícta tu inter mulíeres, et benedíctus fructus ventris tui. Et unde hoc mihi, ut véniat mater Dómini mei ad me? Ecce enim ut facta est vox salutatiónis tuæ in áuribus meis, exsultávit in gáudio infans in útero meo. Et beáta quæ crédidit, quóniam perficiéntur ea, quæ dicta sunt ei a Dómino ». [...]

Mansit autem María cum illa quasi ménsibus tribus et revérsa est in domum suam.[2]

---

[1] *Luke* 1:39-45, 56.
[2] *Lucam* 1, 39-45. 56.

Hail, Mary, full of grace, the Lord is with thee; blessed art thou amongst women, and blessed is the fruit of thy womb, Jesus, **Whom thou didst give birth to**. Holy Mary, Mother of God, pray for us sinners now and at the hour of our death. Amen.

*Ave, María, grátia plena, Dóminus tecum. Benedícta tu in muliéribus, et benedíctus fructus ventris tui, Iesus,* **Quem, Virgo, genuísti**. *Sancta María, Mater Dei, ora pro nobis peccatóribus, nunc et in hora mortis nostræ. Amen.*

## The Third Joyful Mystery
## The Nativity

In those days a decree went out from Caesar Augustus that all the world should be enrolled. [...] And Joseph also went up from Galilee, from the city of Nazareth, to Judea, to the city of David, which is called Bethlehem, because he was of the house and lineage of David, to be enrolled with Mary, his betrothed, who was with child. [...]

And she gave birth to her first-born son and wrapped Him in swaddling cloths, and laid Him in a manger, because there was no place for them in the inn.

And suddenly there was with the angel a multitude of the heavenly host praising God and saying, "Glory to God in the highest, and on earth peace among men with whom He is pleased!"[1]

## Tértium mystérium gaudiósum
## Natívitas

Factum est autem, in diébus illis éxiit edíctum a Cǽsare Augústo, ut describerétur univérsus orbis. [...] Ascéndit autem et Ioseph a Galilǽa de civitáte Názareth in Iudǽam in civitátem David, quæ vocátur Béthlehem, eo quod esset de domo et família David, ut profiterétur cum María desponsáta sibi, uxóre prægnánte. [...]

Et péperit fílium suum primogénitum; et pannis eum invólvit et reclinávit eum in præsépio, quia non erat eis locus in deversório.

Et súbito facta est cum ángelo multitúdo milítiæ cæléstis laudántium Deum et dicéntium: « Glória in altíssimis Deo, et super terram pax in homínibus bonæ voluntátis ».[2]

---
[1] *Luke* 2:1, 4-5, 7, 13-14.
[2] *Lucam* 2, 1. 4-5, 7. 13-14.

Hail, Mary, full of grace, the Lord is with thee; blessed art thou amongst women, and blessed is the fruit of thy womb, Jesus, **Whom thou didst present in the temple**. Holy Mary, Mother of God, pray for us sinners now and at the hour of our death. Amen.

*Ave, María, grátia plena, Dóminus tecum. Benedícta tu in muliéribus, et benedíctus fructus ventris tui, Iesus,* **Quem in templo præsentásti**. *Sancta María, Mater Dei, ora pro nobis peccatóribus, nunc et in hora mortis nostræ. Amen.*

## The Fourth Joyful Mystery
## The Presentation

When the time came for their purification according to the law of Moses, they brought Jesus up to Jerusalem to present Him to the Lord (as it is written in the law of the Lord, "*Every male that opens the womb shall be called holy to the Lord*") and to offer a sacrifice according to what is said in the law of the Lord, *a pair of turtledoves, or two young pigeons.* [...]

And Simeon blessed them and said to Mary His mother, "Behold, this child is set for the fall and rising of many in Israel, and for a sign that is spoken against (and a sword will pierce through your own soul also), that thoughts out of many hearts may be revealed".[1]


## Quartum mystérium gaudiósum
## Præsentátio

Postquam impléti sunt dies purgatiónis eórum secúndum legem Móysis, tulérunt Iesum in Hierosólymam, ut sísterent Dómino, sicut scriptum est in lege Domini: « *Omne masculínum adapériens vulvam sanctum Dómino vocábitur* », et ut darent hóstiam secúndum quod dictum est in lege Dómini: *par túrturum aut duos pullos columbárum.* [...]

Et benedíxit illis Símeon et dixit ad Maríam matrem eius: « Ecce pósitus est hic in ruínam et resurrectiónem multórum in Israel et in signum cui contradicétur—et tuam ipsíus ánimam pertránsiet gládius—ut reveléntur ex multis córdibus cogitatiónes ».[2]

---

[1] *Luke* 2:22-24, 34-35; cf. *Exodus* 13:2, 12; cf. *Leviticus* 12:8.
[2] *Lucam*, 2. 22-24. 34-35; cf. *Exodus* 13, 2. 12; cf. *Leviticus* 12, 8.

Hail, Mary, full of grace, the Lord is with thee; blessed art thou amongst women, and blessed is the fruit of thy womb, Jesus, **Whom thou didst find in the temple**. Holy Mary, Mother of God, pray for us sinners now and at the hour of our death. Amen.

*Ave, María, grátia plena, Dóminus tecum. Benedícta tu in muliéribus, et benedíctus fructus ventris tui, Iesus, **Quem in templo invenísti**. Sancta María, Mater Dei, ora pro nobis peccatóribus, nunc et in hora mortis nostræ. Amen.*

## The Fifth Joyful Mystery
## The Finding in the Temple

Now His parents went to Jerusalem every year at the feast of the Passover. And when He was twelve years old, they went up according to custom; and when the feast was ended, as they were returning, the boy Jesus stayed behind in Jerusalem. His parents did not know it. [...]

After three days they found Him in the temple, sitting among the teachers, listening to them and asking them questions. [...]

And His mother kept all these things in her heart.[1]


## Quintum mystérium gaudiósum
## Invéntio in Templo

Ibant paréntes Iesu per omnes annos in Ierúsalem in die festo Paschæ. Et cum factus esset annórum duódecim, ascendéntibus illis secúndum consuetúdinem diéi festi, consummatísque diébus, cum redírent, remánsit puer Iesus in Ierúsalem, et non cognovérunt paréntes eius. [...]

Et factum est post tríduum invenérunt illum in templo sedéntem in médio doctórum, audiéntem illos et interrogántem eos. [...]

Et Mater eius conservábat ómnia verba in corde suo.[2]

---

[1] *Luke* 2:41-43, 46, 48b-49, 51.
[2] *Lucam* 2, 41-43. 46. 48b-49. 51.

# Mystéria luminósa
## (vel Mysteria lucis)
### in feria quinta

Ab infantia et vita Nazarethana ad publicam Iesu vitam transiens contemplatio ad ea mysteria nos conducit quæ peculiari nomine nuncupari licet « lucis mysteria ». Re quidem vera, totum Christi mysterium lumen est. Ipse est « lux mundi » (*Ioannem* 8, 12). Hæc tamen emergit pars potissimum publicæ vitæ per annos, nuntiante Illo Regni Evangelium...

Annis quidem publicæ vitæ Christi mysterium peculiari titulo demonstratur tamquam lucis mysterium: « Quamdiu in mundo sum, lux sum mundi » (*Ioannem* 9, 5).

S. Ioannes Paulus II

Epistula apostolica *Rosarium Virginis Mariæ*
(16 octobris 2002), nn. 21. 19
*Acta Apostolicae Sedis* 95 (2003) 19. 18

## The Luminous Mysteries
### (or Mysteries of Light)
#### on Thursday[1]

Moving on from the infancy and the hidden life in Nazareth to the public life of Jesus, our contemplation brings us to those mysteries which may be called in a special way "mysteries of light". Certainly the whole mystery of Christ is a mystery of light. He is the "light of the world" (*John* 8:12). Yet this truth emerges in a special way during the years of his public life, when he proclaims the Gospel of the Kingdom...

It is during the years of his public ministry that the mystery of Christ is most evidently a mystery of light: "While I am in the world, I am the light of the world" (*John* 9:5).

St John Paul II

Apostolic Letter *Rosarium Virginis Mariæ*
(16 October 2002), nn. 21 & 19

---

[1] In some places, the Luminous Mysteries (*mystéria luminósa*) are said on 22 October, the liturgical feast of Saint John Paul II, as well as on other days associated with the holy Roman pontiff (2 April, his *dies natalis*, etc.).

Hail, Mary, full of grace, the Lord is with thee; blessed art thou amongst women, and blessed is the fruit of thy womb, Jesus, **Who was baptized in the Jordan**. Holy Mary, Mother of God, pray for us sinners now and at the hour of our death. Amen.

*Ave, María, grátia plena, Dóminus tecum. Benedícta tu in muliéribus, et benedíctus fructus ventris tui, Iesus,* **Qui apud Iordánem baptizátus est**. *Sancta María, Mater Dei, ora pro nobis peccatóribus, nunc et in hora mortis nostræ. Amen.*

## The First Luminous Mystery
## The Baptism in the Jordan

Then Jesus came from Galilee to the Jordan to John, to be baptized by him. John would have prevented Him, saying, "I need to be baptized by You, and do You come to me?"

But Jesus answered him, "Let it be so now; for thus it is fitting for us to fulfil all righteousness". Then he consented.

And when Jesus was baptized, He went up immediately from the water, and behold, the heavens were opened and He saw the Spirit of God descending like a dove, and alighting on Him; and lo, a voice from heaven, saying, "This is My beloved Son, with whom I am well pleased".[1]

## Prímum mystérium lúminis
## Baptísma apud Iordánem

Tunc venit Iesus a Galilaéa in Iordánem ad Ioánnem, ut baptizarétur ab eo. Ioánnes autem prohibébat eum dicens: « Ego a te débeo baptizári, et tu venis ad me? »

Respóndens autem Iesus dixit ei: « Sine modo, sic enim decet nos implére omnem iustítiam ». Tunc dimíttit eum.

Baptizátus autem Iesus, conféstim ascéndit de aqua; et ecce apérti sunt ei cæli, et vidit Spíritum Dei descendéntem sicut colúmbam et veniéntem super se. Et ecce vox de cælis dicens: « Hic est Fílius meus diléctus, in quo mihi complácui ».[2]

---

[1] *Matthew* 3:13-17.
[2] *Matthæum* 3, 13-17.

Hail, Mary, full of grace, the Lord is with thee; blessed art thou amongst women, and blessed is the fruit of thy womb, Jesus, **Who revealed Himself at the wedding feast of Cana**. Holy Mary, Mother of God, pray for us sinners now and at the hour of our death. Amen.

*Ave, María, grátia plena, Dóminus tecum. Benedícta tu in muliéribus, et benedíctus fructus ventris tui, Iesus, **Qui ipsum revelávit apud Canense matrimónium**. Sancta María, Mater Dei, ora pro nobis peccatóribus, nunc et in hora mortis nostræ. Amen.*

## The Second Luminous Mystery
## The Manifestation at the Wedding of Cana

On the third day there was a marriage at Cana in Galilee, and the mother of Jesus was there; Jesus also was invited to the marriage, with his disciples. When the wine failed, the mother of Jesus said to him, "They have no wine". And Jesus said to her, "O woman, what have you to do with Me? My hour has not yet come". His mother said to the servants, "Do whatever He tells you". [...] Jesus said to them, "Fill the jars with water". [...]

When the steward of the feast tasted the water now become wine, and did not know where it came from [...], the steward of the feast called the bridegroom and said to him, "Every man serves the good wine first; and when men have drunk freely, then the poor wine; but you have kept the good wine until now".[1]

## Secúndum mystérium lúminis
## Autorevelátio apud Cananénse matrimónium

Núptiæ factæ sunt in Cana Galilǽæ, et erat mater Iesu ibi; vocátus est autem et Iesus et discípuli eius ad núptias. Et deficiénte vino, dicit mater Iesu ad eum: « Vinum non habent ». Et dicit ei Iesus: « Quid mihi et tibi, múlier? Nondum venit hora mea ». Dicit mater eius minístris: « Quodcúmque díxerit vobis, fácite ». [...] Dicit eis Iesus: « Impléte hýdrias aqua ». [...]

Ut autem gustávit architriclínus aquam vinum factam et non sciébat unde esset [...], vocat sponsum architriclínus et dicit ei: « Omnis homo primum bonum vinum ponit et, cum inebriáti fúerint, id quod detérius est; tu servásti bonum vinum usque adhuc ».[2]

---

[1] *John* 2:1-5, 7a, 9-10.
[2] *Ioannem* 2, 1-5, 7a, 9-10.

Hail, Mary, full of grace, the Lord is with thee; blessed art thou amongst women, and blessed is the fruit of thy womb, Jesus, **Who announced the Kingdom of God**. Holy Mary, Mother of God, pray for us sinners now and at the hour of our death. Amen.

*Ave, María, grátia plena, Dóminus tecum. Benedícta tu in muliéribus, et benedíctus fructus ventris tui, Iesus, **Qui Regnum Dei annuntiávit**. Sancta Maria, Mater Dei, ora pro nobis peccatóribus, nunc et in hora mortis nostræ. Amen.*

## The Third Luminous Mystery
## The Proclamation of the Kingdom of God
### and the subsequent Call to Conversion

Now when Jesus heard that John had been arrested, He withdrew into Galilee; and leaving Nazareth He went and dwelt in Capernaum by the sea, in the territory of Zebulun and Naphtali, that what was spoken by the prophet Isaiah might be fulfilled:

"*The land of Zebulun and the land of Naphtali, toward the sea, across the Jordan, Galilee of the Gentiles— the people who sat in darkness have seen a great light, and for those who sat in the region and shadow of death light has dawned*".

From that time Jesus began to preach, saying, "Repent, for the kingdom of heaven is at hand".[1]

## Tértium mystérium lúminis
## Regni Dei proclamátio
### coniúncta cum invitaménto ad conversiónem

Cum audísset Iesus quod Ioánnes tráditus esset, secéssit in Galilǽam. Et relícta Názareth, venit et habitávit in Caphárnaum marítimam in fínibus Zábulon et Néphtali, ut implerétur, quod dictum est per Isaíam prophétam dicéntem:

« *Terra Zábulon et terra Néphtali, ad viam maris, trans Iordánem, Galilǽa géntium; pópulus, qui sedébat in ténebris, lucem vidit magnam, et sedéntibus in regióne et umbra mortis lux orta est eis* ».

Exínde cœpit Iesus prædicáre et dícere: « Pæniténtiam ágite; appropinquávit enim regnum cælórum ».[2]

---
[1] *Matthew* 4:12-17; cf. *Isaiah* 8:23; 9:1.
[2] *Matthæum* 4, 12-17; cf. *Isaiæ* 8, 23; 9, 1.

Hail, Mary, full of grace, the Lord is with thee; blessed art thou amongst women, and blessed is the fruit of thy womb, Jesus, **Who was transfigured**. Holy Mary, Mother of God, pray for us sinners now and at the hour of our death. Amen.

*Ave, María, grátia plena, Dóminus tecum. Benedícta tu in muliéribus, et benedíctus fructus ventris tui, Iesus, **Qui transfigurátus est**. Sancta María, Mater Dei, ora pro nobis peccatóribus, nunc et in hora mortis nostræ. Amen.*

## The Fourth Luminous Mystery
## The Transfiguration

Jesus took with Him Peter and James and John his brother, and led them up a high mountain apart. And He was transfigured before them, and His face shone like the sun, and His garments became white as light And behold, there appeared to them Moses and Elijah, talking with Him.

And Peter said to Jesus, "Lord, it is well that we are here; if You wish, I will make three booths here, one for You and one for Moses and one for Elijah".

He was still speaking, when behold, a bright cloud overshadowed them, and a voice from the cloud said, "This is My beloved Son, with Whom I am well pleased; listen to Him".[1]

## Quartum mystérium lúminis
## Transfigurátio

Assúmit Iesus Petrum et Iacóbum et Ioánnem fratrem eius et ducit illos in montem excélsum seórsum. Et transfigurátus est ante eos; et respénduit fácies eius sicut sol, vestiménta autem eius facta sunt alba sicut lux. Et ecce appáruit illis Móyses et Elías cum eo loquéntes.

Respóndens autem Petrus dixit ad Iesum: « Dómine, bonum est nos hic esse. Si vis, fáciam hic tria tabernácula: tibi unum et Móysi unum et Elíæ unum ».

Adhuc eo loquénte, ecce nubes lúcida obumbrávit eos; et ecce vox de nube dicens: « Hic est Fílius meus diléctus, in quo mihi bene complácui; ipsum audíte ».[2]

---

[1] *Matthew* 17:1-5.
[2] *Mattæum* 17, 1-5.

Hail, Mary, full of grace, the Lord is with thee; blessed art thou amongst women, and blessed is the fruit of thy womb, Jesus, **Who instituted the Eucharist**. Holy Mary, Mother of God, pray for us sinners now and at the hour of our death. Amen.

*Ave, María, grátia plena, Dóminus tecum. Benedícta tu in muliéribus, et benedíctus fructus ventris tui, Iesus, **Qui Eucharístiam instítuit**. Sancta María, Mater Dei, ora pro nobis peccatóribus, nunc et in hora mortis nostræ. Amen.*

## The Fifth Luminous Mystery
## The Institution of the Eucharist

And as they were eating, He took bread, and blessed, and broke it, and gave it to them, and said, "Take; this is My body". And He took a chalice, and when He had given thanks He gave it to them, and they all drank of it. And He said to them, "This is My blood of the covenant, which is poured out for many".[1]

"Truly, truly, I say to you, unless you eat the flesh of the Son of man and drink His blood, you have no life in you; he who eats My flesh and drinks My blood has eternal life, and I will raise him up at the last day. For My flesh is food indeed, and My blood is drink indeed. He who eats my flesh and drinks My blood abides in Me, and I in him".[2]

## Quintum mystérium lúminis
## Eucharístiæ Institútio

Et manducántibus illis, accépit panem et benedícens fregit et dedit eis et ait: « Súmite: hoc est corpus meum ». Et accépto cálice, grátias agens dedit eis, et bibérunt ex illo omnes. Et ait illis: « Hic est sanguis meus novi testaménti, qui pro multis effúnditur ».[3]

« Amen, amen dico vobis: Nisi manducavéritis carnem Fílii hóminis et bibéritis eius sánguinem, non habétis vitam in vobismetípsis. Qui mandúcat meam carnem et bibit meum sánguinem, habet vitam ætérnam; et ego resuscitábo eum in novíssimo die Caro enim mea verus est cibus, et sanguis meus verus est potus. Qui mandúcat meam carnem et bibit meum sánguinem, in me manet, et ego in illo ».[4]

---

[1] *Mark* 14:22-24.
[2] *John* 6:53-56.
[3] *Marcum* 14, 22-24.
[4] *Ioannem* 6, 53-56.

## Mystéria dolorósa

### in feria tertia et feria sexta

Magnum quidem pondus Christi mysteriis doloris tribuunt Evangelia. A primis iam temporibus christiana pietas, præsertim Quadragesimæ tempore, per pium Viæ Crucis usum, singulis commoratur in Passionis eventibus, quoniam hic revelationis amoris ipsum culmen esse intellegit et hic etiam salutis nostræ originem. Quædam dumtaxat Passionis momenta eligit Rosarium in quæ precantem movet ut animi oculos convertat et eadem vivat...

Ecce homo: qui hominem cognoscere cupit, eiusdem hominis sensum radicem complementum agnoscere debet in Christo, Deo nempe illo qui ex amore humiliavit semetipsum « usque ad mortem, mortem autem crucis » (*Philippenses* 2, 8). Adducunt credentem doloris mysteria ut Iesu mortem iterum vivendo experiatur seque iuxta Mariam infra crucem collocet, ut in profundum Dei amorem erga homines cum Ea pervadat omnemque illius percipiat regenerantem virtutem.

S. IOANNES PAULUS II

Epistula apostolica *Rosarium Virginis Mariæ*
(16 octobris 2002), n. 22:
*Acta Apostolicae Sedis* 95 (2003) 21

## The Sorrowful Mysteries

on Tuesday and Friday[1]

The Gospels give great prominence to the sorrowful mysteries of Christ. From the beginning Christian piety, especially during the Lenten devotion of the Way of the Cross, has focused on the individual moments of the Passion, realizing that here is found the culmination of the revelation of God's love and the source of our salvation. The Rosary selects certain moments from the Passion, inviting the faithful to contemplate them in their hearts and to relive them...

*Ecce homo:* the meaning, origin and fulfilment of man is to be found in Christ, the God who humbles himself out of love "even unto death, death on a cross" (*Philippians* 2:8). The sorrowful mysteries help the believer to relive the death of Jesus, to stand at the foot of the Cross beside Mary, to enter with her into the depths of God's love for man and to experience all its life-giving power.

St John Paul II

Apostolic Letter *Rosarium Virginis Mariæ*
(16 October 2002), n. 22

---

[1] In some places, the Sorrowful Mysteries (*mystéria dolorósa*) are said daily during Lent (*Quadragesima*).

Hail, Mary, full of grace, the Lord is with thee; blessed art thou amongst women, and blessed is the fruit of thy womb, Jesus, **Who sweated bood for us**. Holy Mary, Mother of God, pray for us sinners now and at the hour of our death. Amen.

*Ave, María, grátia plena, Dóminus tecum. Benedícta tu in muliéribus, et benedíctus fructus ventris tui, Iesus,* **Qui pro nobis sánguinem sudávit***. Sancta María, Mater Dei, ora pro nobis peccatóribus, nunc et in hora mortis nostræ. Amen.*

## The First Sorrowful Mystery
## The Agony in the Garden

And He came out, and went, as was His custom, to the Mount of Olives; and the disciples followed Him. [...]

And He withdrew from them about a stone's throw, and knelt down and prayed, "Father, if Thou art willing, remove this chalice from Me; nevertheless not My will, but Thine, be done". And there appeared to Him an angel from heaven, strengthening Him. And being in an agony He prayed more earnestly; and His sweat became like great drops of blood falling down upon the ground.

And when He rose from prayer, He came to the disciples and found them sleeping for sorrow, and He said to them, "Why do you sleep? Rise and pray that you may not enter into temptation".[1]


## Prímum mystérium dolorósum
## Agonía in Hortu

Et egréssus ibat secúndum consuetúdinem in montem Olivárum; secúti sunt autem illum et discípuli. [...]

Et ipse avúlsus est ab eis, quantum iactus est lápidis, et, pósitis génibus, orábat dicens: « Pater, si vis, transfer cálicem istum a me; verúmtamen non mea volúntas sed tua fiat ». Appáruit autem illi ángelus de cælo confórtans eum. Et factus in agonía, prolíxius orábat. Et factus est sudor eius sicut guttæ sánguinis decurréntis in terram.

Et cum surrexísset ab oratióne et venísset ad discípulos, invénit eos dormiéntes præ tristítia et ait illis: « Quid dormítis? Súrgite; oráte, ne intrétis in tentatiónem ».[2]

---
[1] *Luke* 22:39, 41-46.
[2] *Lucam* 22, 39. 41-46.

Hail, Mary, full of grace, the Lord is with thee; blessed art thou amongst women, and blessed is the fruit of thy womb, Jesus, **Who was scourged for us**. Holy Mary, Mother of God, pray for us sinners now and at the hour of our death. Amen.

*Ave, María, grátia plena, Dóminus tecum. Benedícta tu in muliéribus, et benedíctus fructus ventris tui, Iesus, **Qui pro nobis flagellátus est**. Sancta María, Mater Dei, ora pro nobis peccatóribus, nunc et in hora mortis nostræ. Amen.*

## The Second Sorrowful Mystery
## The Scourging

And Pilate again said to them, "Then what shall I do with the man whom you call the King of the Jews?" And they cried out again, "Crucify Him". And Pilate said to them, "Why, what evil has He done?" But they shouted all the more, "Crucify Him".

So Pilate, wishing to satisfy the crowd, released for them Barabbas; and having scourged Jesus, he delivered Him to be crucified.[1]

*He was despised and rejected by men; a man of sorrows, and acquainted with grief; and as one from whom men hide their faces He was despised, and we esteemed Him not.*[2]

## Secúndum mystérium dolorósum
## Flagellátio

Pilátus autem íterum respóndens aiébat illis: « Quid ergo vultis fáciam regi Iudæórum? » At illi íterum clamavérunt: « Crucifíge eum! » Pilátus vero dicébat eis: « Quid enim mali fecit? » At illi magis clamavérunt: « Crucifíge eum! »

Pilátus autem, volens pópulo satisfácere, dimísit illis Barábbam et trádidit Iesum flagéllis cæsum, ut crucifigerétur ».[3]

*Despéctus erat et novíssimus virórum, vir dolórum et sciens infirmitátem, et quasi abscondebámus vultum coram eo; despéctus, unde nec reputabámus eum.*[4]

---

[1] *Mark* 15:12-15.
[2] *Isaiah* 53:3.
[3] *Marcum* 15, 12-15.
[4] *Isaiæ* 53, 3.

Hail, Mary, full of grace, the Lord is with thee; blessed art thou amongst women, and blessed is the fruit of thy womb, Jesus, **Who was crowned with thorns for us**. Holy Mary, Mother of God, pray for us sinners now and at the hour of our death. Amen.

*Ave, María, grátia plena, Dóminus tecum. Benedícta tu in muliéribus, et benedíctus fructus ventris tui, Iesus,* **Qui pro nobis spinis coronátus est**. *Sancta María, Mater Dei, ora pro nobis peccatóribus, nunc et in hora mortis nostræ. Amen.*

## The Third Sorrowful Mystery
## The Crowning with Thorns

Then the soldiers of the governor took Jesus into the praetorium, and they gathered the whole battalion before Him. And they stripped Him and put a scarlet robe upon Him, and plaiting a crown of thorns they put it on His head, and put a reed in His right hand. And kneeling before Him they mocked Him, saying, "Hail, King of the Jews!"[1]

*Surely He has borne our griefs and carried our sorrows; yet we esteemed Him stricken, struck down by God, and afflicted. But He was wounded for our transgressions, He was bruised for our iniquities; upon Him was the chastisement that made us whole, and with His stripes we are healed.*[2]

## Tertium mystérium dolorósum
## Coronátio Spinis

Tunc mílites præsidis suscipiéntes Iesum in prætório congregavérunt ad eum univérsam cohórtem. Et exuéntes eum, clámydem coccíneam circumdedérunt ei et plecténtes corónam de spinis posuérunt super caput eius et arúndinem in déxtera eius et, genu flexo ante eum, illudébant ei dicéntes: « Ave, rex Iudæórum! »[3]

*Vere languóres nostros ipse tulit et dolóres nostros ipse portávit; et nos putávimus eum quasi plagátum, et percússum a Deo et humiliátum. Ipse autem vulnerátus est propter iniquitátes nostras, attrítus est propter scélera nostra; disciplína pacis nostræ super eum, et livóre eius sanáti sumus.*[4]

---

[1] *Matthew* 27:27-29.
[2] *Isaiah* 53:4-5.
[3] *Matthæum* 27, 27-29.
[4] *Isaiæ* 53, 4-5.

Hail, Mary, full of grace, the Lord is with thee; blessed art thou amongst women, and blessed is the fruit of thy womb, Jesus, **Who carried the Cross for us**. Holy Mary, Mother of God, pray for us sinners now and at the hour of our death. Amen.

*Ave, María, grátia plena, Dóminus tecum. Benedícta tu in muliéribus, et benedíctus fructus ventris tui, Iesus,* **Qui pro nobis crucem baiulávit**. *Sancta María, Mater Dei, ora pro nobis peccatóribus, nunc et in hora mortis nostræ. Amen.*

## The Fourth Sorrowful Mystery
## The Carrying of the Cross

And as they led Him away, they seized one Simon of Cyrene, who was coming in from the country, and laid on him the cross, to carry it behind Jesus.

And there followed Him a great multitude of the people, and of women who bewailed and lamented Him. But Jesus turning to them said, "Daughters of Jerusalem, do not weep for Me, but weep for yourselves and for your children. For behold, the days are coming when they will say, 'Blessed are the barren, and the wombs that never bore, and the breasts that never nursed!'

"Then they will begin *to say to the mountains, 'Fall on us'; and to the hills, 'Cover us'*. For if they do this when the wood is green, what will happen when it is dry?"[1]

## Quartum mystérium dolorósum
## Baiulátio Crucis

Et cum abdúcerent eum, apprehendérunt Simónem quemdam Cyrenénsem veniéntem de villa et imposuérunt illi crucem portáre post Iesum.

Sequebátur autem illum multa turba pópuli et mulíerum, quæ plangébant et lamentábant eum. Convérsus autem ad illas Iesus dixit: « Fíliæ Ierúsalem, nolíte flere super me, sed super vos ipsas flete et super fílios vestros, quóniam ecce vénient dies, in quibus dicent: "Beátæ stériles et ventres, qui non genuérunt, et úbera quæ non lactavérunt!".

« Tunc incípient *dícere móntibus: "Cádite super nos!"*, *et cóllibus: "Operíte nos!"*, quia si in víridi ligno hæc fáciunt, in árido quid fiet? ».[2]

---

[1] *Luke* 23:26-31; cf. *Hosea* 10:8.

[2] *Lucam* 23, 26-31; cf. *Osee* 10, 8.

Hail, Mary, full of grace, the Lord is with thee; blessed art thou amongst women, and blessed is the fruit of thy womb, Jesus, **Who was crucified for us**. Holy Mary, Mother of God, pray for us sinners now and at the hour of our death. Amen.

*Ave, María, grátia plena, Dóminus tecum. Benedícta tu in muliéribus, et benedíctus fructus ventris tui, Iesus,* ***Qui pro nobis crucifíxus est****. Sancta María, Mater Dei, ora pro nobis peccatóribus, nunc et in hora mortis nostræ. Amen.*

## The Fifth Sorrowful Mystery
## The Crucifixion and Death on the Cross

And when they had crucified Him, they *divided His garments among them by casting lots*. [...] And over His head they put the charge against Him, which read, "This is Jesus the King of the Jews".

Now from the sixth hour there was darkness over all the land until the ninth hour. And about the ninth hour Jesus cried with a loud voice: "*My God, My God, why hast Thou forsaken Me?*"

And Jesus cried again with a loud voice and yielded up His spirit. And behold, the curtain of the temple was torn in two, from top to bottom; and the earth shook, and the rocks were split...[1]

## Quintum mystérium dolorósum
## Crucifíxio et Mors in Cruce

Postquam autem crucifixérunt eum, *divisérunt vestiménta eius sortem mitténtes.* [...] Et imposuérunt super caput eius causam ipsíus scriptam: « Hic est Iesus Rex Iudæórum ».

A sexta autem hora tenébræ factæ sunt super univérsam terram usque ad horam nonam. Et circa horam nonam clamávit Iesus voce magna dicens: « *Deus meus, Deus meus, ut quid dereliquísti me?* »

Iesus autem íterum clamans voce magna emísit spíritum. Et ecce velum templi scissum est a summo usque deórsum in duas partes, et terra mota est, et petræ scissæ sunt...[2]

---

[1] *Matthew* 27:35, 37, 45-46, 50-51; cf. *Psalm* 22:18, 1.
[2] *Matthæum* 27, 35. 37. 45-46. 50-51; cf. *Psalmus* 21, 19. 2 (Vulgata).

## Mystéria gloriósa

### in feria quarta et Dominica

« Sistere haud potest eius Christi vultus contemplatio ad Ipsius cruci adfixi imaginem. Etenim est Ille Resuscitatus! » (*Novo millennio ineunte*, 28). Iam hanc fidei conscientiam semper exprimit Rosarium cum credentes incitat ut ultra Passionis obscuritatem procedant suosque animos in Christi gloriam Resurrectionis et Ascensionis dirigant. Resuscitatum enim Dominum contemplans suæ causas fidei detegit iterum christianus (cfr. *I Corinthios* 15, 14) ...

Sic enim in credentibus nutriunt mysteria gloriosa metæ eschatologicæ spem ad quam uti Populi Dei per historiam peregrinantis membra progrediuntur. Hoc facere non potest quin eos ad animosam impellat illius « læti nuntii » testificationem quæ omni eorum vitæ significationem adiungit.

S. IOANNES PAULUS II

Epistula apostolica *Rosarium Virginis Mariæ*
(16 octobris 2002), n. 23
*Acta Apostolicae Sedis* 95 (2003) 22

# The Glorious Mysteries
on Wednesday and Sunday[1]

"The contemplation of Christ's face cannot stop at the image of the Crucified One. He is the Risen One!" (*Novo Millennio Ineunte*, 28). The Rosary has always expressed this knowledge born of faith and invited the believer to pass beyond the darkness of the Passion in order to gaze upon Christ's glory in the Resurrection and Ascension. Contemplating the Risen One, Christians rediscover the reasons for their own faith (cf. *1 Corinthians* 15:14) ...

The glorious mysteries thus lead the faithful to greater hope for the eschatological goal towards which they journey as members of the pilgrim People of God in history. This can only impel them to bear courageous witness to that "good news" which gives meaning to their entire existence.

St John Paul II

Apostolic Letter *Rosarium Virginis Mariæ*
(16 October 2002), n. 23

---

[1] For those who do not observe the Luminous Mysteries (*mystéria luminósa*), the Glorious Mysteries (*mystéria gloriósa*) are said on Wednesday and Saturday. In some places, the Glorious Mysteries (*mystéria gloriósa*) are said daily during the Octave of Easter (*Octava Paschæ*).

Hail, Mary, full of grace, the Lord is with thee; blessed art thou amongst women, and blessed is the fruit of thy womb, Jesus, **Who rose from the dead**. Holy Mary, Mother of God, pray for us sinners now and at the hour of our death. Amen.

*Ave, María, grátia plena, Dóminus tecum. Benedícta tu in muliéribus, et benedíctus fructus ventris tui, Iesus, **Qui resurréxit a mórtuis**. Sancta María, Mater Dei, ora pro nobis peccatóribus, nunc et in hora mortis nostræ. Amen.*

## The First Glorious Mystery
## The Resurrection

When the sabbath was past, Mary Magdalene, and Mary the mother of James, and Salome, bought spices, so that they might go and anoint Him. And very early on the first day of the week they went to the tomb when the sun had risen.

And they were saying to one another, "Who will roll away the stone for us from the door of the tomb?"And looking up, they saw that the stone was rolled back;— it was very large.

And entering the tomb, they saw a young man sitting on the right side, dressed in a white robe; and they were amazed. And he said to them, "Do not be amazed; you seek Jesus of Nazareth, who was crucified. He has risen, He is not here; see the place where they laid Him".[1]

## Prímum mystérium gloriósum
## Resurréctio

Cum transísset sábbatum, María Magdaléne et María Iacóbi et Salóme emérunt arómata, ut veniéntes úngerent eum. Et valde mane, prima sabbatórum, véniunt ad monuméntum, orto iam sole.

Et dicébant ad ínvicem: « Quis revólvet nobis lápidem ab óstio monuménti? » Et respiciéntes vident revolútum lápidem; erat quippe magnus valde.

Et introeúntes in monuméntum vidérunt iúvenem sedéntem in dextris, coopértum stola cándida, et obstupuérunt. Qui dicit illis: « Nolíte expavéscere! Iesum quǽritis Nazarénum crucifíxum. Surréxit, non est hic; ecce locus, ubi posuérunt eum ».[2]

---
[1] *Mark* 16:1-6.
[2] *Marcum* 16, 5-6.

Hail, Mary, full of grace, the Lord is with thee; blessed art thou amongst women, and blessed is the fruit of thy womb, Jesus, **Who ascended into heaven**. Holy Mary, Mother of God, pray for us sinners now and at the hour of our death. Amen.

*Ave, María, grátia plena, Dóminus tecum. Benedícta tu in muliéribus, et benedíctus fructus ventris tui, Iesus,* **Qui in cælum ascéndit**. *Sancta María, Mater Dei, ora pro nobis peccatóribus, nunc et in hora mortis nostræ. Amen.*

## The Second Glorious Mystery
## The Ascension

And while staying with them He charged them not to depart from Jerusalem, but to wait for the promise of the Father, which, He said, "you heard from Me, for John baptized with water, but before many days you shall be baptized with the Holy Spirit". [...]

And when He had said this, as they were looking on, He was lifted up, and a cloud took Him out of their sight.

And while they were gazing into heaven as He went, behold, two men stood by them in white robes, and said, "Men of Galilee, why do you stand looking into heaven? This Jesus, who was taken up from you into heaven, will come in the same way as you saw Him go into heaven".[1]

## Secúndum mystérium gloriósum
## Ascénsio

Et convéscens præcépit eis ab Hierosólymis ne discéderent, sed exspectárent promissiónem Patris: « Quam audístis a me, quia Ioánnes quidem baptizávit aqua, vos autem baptizabímini in Spíritu Sancto non post multos hos dies ». [...]

Et cum hæc dixísset, vidéntibus illis, elevátus est, et nubes suscépit eum ab óculis eórum.

Cumque intueréntur in cælum, eúnte illo, ecce duo viri astitérunt iuxta illos in véstibus albis, qui et dixérunt: « Viri Galilǽi, quid statis aspiciéntes in cælum? Hic Iesus, qui assúmptus est a vobis in cælum, sic véniet quemádmodum vidístis eum eúntem in cælum ».[2]

---

[1] *Acts* 1:4-5, 9-11.
[2] *Act* 1, 4-5. 9-11.

Hail, Mary, full of grace, the Lord is with thee; blessed art thou amongst women, and blessed is the fruit of thy womb, Jesus, **Who sent the Holy Spirit**. Holy Mary, Mother of God, pray for us sinners now and at the hour of our death. Amen.

*Ave, María, grátia plena, Dóminus tecum. Benedícta tu in muliéribus, et benedíctus fructus ventris tui, Iesus,* **Qui Spíritum Sanctum misit**. *Sancta María, Mater Dei, ora pro nobis peccatóribus, nunc et in hora mortis nostræ. Amen.*

## The Third Glorious Mystery
## The Descent of the Holy Spirit

When the day of Pentecost had come, they were all together in one place. And suddenly a sound came from heaven like the rush of a mighty wind, and it filled all the house where they were sitting. And there appeared to them tongues as of fire, distributed and resting on each one of them. And they were all filled with the Holy Spirit and began to speak in other tongues, as the Spirit gave them utterance.

Now there were dwelling in Jerusalem Jews, devout men from every nation under heaven. And at this sound the multitude came together, and they were bewildered, because each one heard them speaking in his own language.[1]

## Tértium mystérium gloriósum
## Descénsus Spíritus Sancti

Cum complerétur dies Pentecóstes, erant omnes páriter in eódem loco. Et factus est repénte de cælo sonus tamquam adveniéntis spíritus veheméntis et replévit totam domum, ubi erant sedéntes. Et apparuérunt illis dispertítæ linguæ tamquam ignis, sedítque supra síngulos eórum; et repléti sunt omnes Spíritu Sancto et cœpérunt loqui áliis linguis, prout Spíritus dabat éloqui illis.

Erant autem in Ierúsalem habitántes Iudǽi, viri religiósi ex omni natióne, quæ sub cælo est; facta autem hac voce, convénit multitúdo et confúsa est, quóniam audiébat unusquísque lingua sua illos loquéntes.[2]

---

[1] *Acts* 2:1-6.
[2] *Act* 2, 1-6.

Hail, Mary, full of grace, the Lord is with thee; blessed art thou amongst women, and blessed is the fruit of thy womb, Jesus, **Who assumed thee into heaven**. Holy Mary, Mother of God, pray for us sinners now and at the hour of our death. Amen.

*Ave, María, grátia plena, Dóminus tecum. Benedícta tu in muliéribus, et benedíctus fructus ventris tui, Iesus,* ***Qui te assúmpsit****. Sancta María, Mater Dei, ora pro nobis peccatóribus, nunc et in hora mortis nostræ. Amen.*

## The Fourth Glorious Mystery
## The Assumption of the Blessed Virgin Mary

Elizabeth was filled with the Holy Spirit and she exclaimed with a loud cry, "Blessed are you among women, and blessed is the fruit of your womb! [...] And blessed is she who believed that there would be a fulfilment of what was spoken to her from the Lord."

And Mary said, "*My soul* magnifies *the Lord*, and my spirit *rejoices in God my Savior*, for he has *regarded* the *low estate* of his *handmaiden*. For behold, henceforth all generations will call me blessed".[1]

And a great portent appeared in heaven, a woman clothed with the sun, with the moon under her feet, and on her head a crown of twelve stars.[2]

## Quartum mystérium gloriósum
## Assúmptio Beátæ Maríæ Vírginis

Repléta est Spíritu Sancto Elísabeth et exclamávit voce magna et dixit: « Benedícta tu inter mulíeres, et benedíctus fructus ventris tui. [...] Et beáta quæ crédidit, quóniam perficiéntur ea, quæ dicta sunt ei a Dómino ».

Et ait María: « Magníficat *ánima mea Dóminum*, et *exsultávit* spíritus meus *in Deo salvatóre meo*, quia *respéxit humilitátem ancíllæ* suæ. Ecce enim ex hoc beátam me dicent omnes generatiónes ».[3]

Et signum magnum appáruit in cælo: múlier amícta sole, et luna sub pédibus eius, et super caput eius coróna stellárum duódecim.[4]

---

[1] *Luke* 1:41b-42, 45-48; cf. *1 Samuel* 2:1-10 and *Habakkuk* 3:18.
[2] *The Apocalypse* 12:1.
[3] *Lucam* 1, 41b-42, 45-48; cf. *I Samuelis* 2, 1-10 et *Habacuc* 3, 18.
[4] *Apocalypsis Ioannis* 12, 1.

Hail, Mary, full of grace, the Lord is with thee; blessed art thou amongst women, and blessed is the fruit of thy womb, Jesus, **Who crowned thee Queen of heaven**. Holy Mary, Mother of God, pray for us sinners now and at the hour of our death. Amen.

*Ave, María, grátia plena, Dóminus tecum. Benedícta tu in muliéribus, et benedíctus fructus ventris tui, Iesus,* ***Qui te in cælis coronávit****. Sancta María, Mater Dei, ora pro nobis peccatóribus, nunc et in hora mortis nostræ. Amen.*

## The Fifth Glorious Mystery
## The Coronation in Heaven

The angel Gabriel was sent from God to a city of Galilee named Nazareth, to a virgin betrothed to a man whose name was Joseph, of the house of David; and the virgin's name was Mary. And he came to her and said, "Hail, full of grace, the Lord is with you! [...]

"Behold, you will conceive in your womb and bear a son, and you shall call His name Jesus. He will be great, and will be called the Son of the Most High; and the Lord God will give to Him the throne of His father David, and He will reign over the house of Jacob for ever; and of His kingdom there will be no end".[1]

*Come: thou shalt be crowned...*[2]

## Quintum mystérium gloriósum
## Coronátio in Cælo

Missus est ángelus Gábriel a Deo in civitátem Galilǽæ, cui nomen Názareth, ad vírginem desponsátam viro, cui nomen erat Ioseph de domo David, et nomen vírginis María. Et ingréssus ad eam dixit: « Ave, grátia plena, Dóminus tecum [...]

« Ecce concípies in útero et páries fílium, et vocábis nomen eius Iesum. Hic erit magnus et Fílius Altíssimi vocábitur, et dabit illi Dóminus Deus sedem David patris eius, et regnábit super domum Iacob in ætérnum, et regni eius non erit finis ».[3]

*Veni, coronáberis.*[4]

---

[1] *Luke* 1:26-28, 31-33.
[2] *Song of Songs* 4:8; Douay-Rheims, 1899 American Edition.
[3] *Lucam* 1, 26-28, 31-33.
[4] *Canticum Canticorum* 4, 8; 1592 Clementine Vulgate.

# Appendices

*"The holy Rosary is a powerful weapon.
Use it with confidence
and you'll be amazed at the results".*

SAINT JOSEMARÍA ESCRIVÁ DE BALAGUER
1902-1975

# I
# Orationes variæ

### Antiphona

Sub tuum præsídium confúgimus,
sancta Dei Génetrix;
nostras deprecatiónes ne despícias in necessitátibus:
sed a perículis cunctis líbera nos semper,
Virgo gloriósa et benedícta.

### Oratio

Memoráre, o piíssima Virgo María,
non esse audítum a sǽculo,
quemquam ad tua curréntem præsídia,
tua implorántem auxília,
tua peténtem suffrágia, esse derelíctum.
Ego tali animátus confidéntia, ad te,
Virgo Vírginum, Mater,
curro, ad te vénio,
coram te gemens peccátor assísto.
Noli, Mater Verbi,
verba mea despícere;
sed áudi propítia et exáudi. Amen.

Ter:

℣. O María sine labe concépta.
℟. Ora pro nobis, qui confugimus ad te.

### Invocationes

Dignáre me laudáre te, Virgo sacráta;
da mihi virtútem contra hostes tuos.

Mater mea, líbera me a peccáto mortáli.

Sancta María, líbera nos a pœnis inférni.

Virgo Dei Génitrix, María, deprecáre Iesum pro me.

O María, fac ut vivam in Deo,
cum Deo et pro Deo.

# I
# Various Prayers

### ANTIPHON

We fly to your protection,
O holy Mother of God;
despise not our petitions in our necessities,
but deliver us always from all dangers,
O glorious and blessed Virgin.

### PRAYER

Remember, O Most Gracious Virgin Mary,
that never was it known
that anyone who fled to thy protection,
implored thy help
or sought thy intercession was left unaided.
Inspired with this confidence, I fly unto thee,
O Virgin of virgins, my Mother;
to thee do I come, before thee I stand,
sinful and sorrowful;
O Mother of the Word Incarnate,
despise not my petitions,
but in thy mercy hear and answer me. Amen.

Thrice:

℣. O Mary conceived without sin.
℟. Pray for us, who have recourse to thee.

### INVOCATIONS

Vouchsafe that I may praise thee, O sacred Virgin;
give me strength against thine enemies.

My Mother, deliver me from mortal sin.

Holy Mary, deliver us from the pains of hell.

O Mary, Virgin Mother of God, pray to Jesus for me.

O Mary, make me to live in God,
with God, and for God.

## Hymn[1]

O Queen of the Holy Rosary,
Oh, bless us as we pray,
And offer thee our roses
In garlands day by day,
While from our Father's garden,
With loving hearts and bold,
We gather to thine honour
Buds white and red and gold.

O Queen of the Holy Rosary,
Each myst'ry blends with thine
The sacred life of Jesus
In ev'ry step divine,
Thy soul was His fair garden,
Thy virgin breast His throne,
Thy thoughts His faithful mirror,
Reflecting Him alone.

O Queen of the Holy Rosary,
We share thy joy and pain,
And long to see the glory
Of Christ's triumphant reign.
Oh, teach us holy Mary,
To live each mystery,
And gain by patient suff'ring
The glory won by thee.

Another appropriate hymn may be sung.

---

[1] Emily M. Shapcote, d.c. 1906, & Fr Irvin, OFM Cap. *Wirtemburg Gesangbuch*, 1784 (T.C.K): *The New Saint Basil Hymnal* (1958), n. 157; p. 178.

## Prayer Before the Rosary
*by* Saint Louis Marie de Montfort

I unite with all the saints in heaven, with all the just on earth |and with all the faithful here present|. I unite with You, my Jesus, in order to praise Your holy Mother worthily and to praise You in her and through her. I renounce all distractions which may arise during this Rosary. I desire to say it with attention and devotion as if it were the last of my life. Amen.

We offer You, O most Holy Trinity, this Creed in honor of all the mysteries of our Faith; this Our Father and these three Hail Marys in honor of the unity of Your Essence and the Trinity of Your Persons. We ask of You a lively faith, a firm hope, and an ardent charity. Amen.

## Another Prayer Before the Rosary

Queen of the Holy Rosary,
you have deigned to come to Fatima
to reveal to the three shepherd children
the treasures of grace hidden in the Rosary.

Inspire my heart
with a sincere love of this devotion,
in order that by meditating
on the Mysteries of our Redemption
which are recalled in it,
I may be enriched with its fruits
and obtain peace for the world,
|the conversion of Russia,|
and the favour which I ask of you in this Rosary.

(Here mention your request.)

I ask it for the greater glory of God,
for your own honour,
and for the good of souls,
especially for my own. Amen.

# II
# The Rosary Novena
## *Novendiales*

A novena (*novendiales*) is a public or private devotion repeated nine successive times. The succession may consist of continous days (nine days before a feast), or specific days of the week (nine Mondays), or specific days of the month (nine first Fridays, etc.). Novenas may be for special intentions and may be repeated without limit.

The origin of the novena goes back to the nine days that the Holy Virgin Mary and the apostles spent in prayer between the Ascension Thursday and Pentecost Sunday (cf. *Acts of the Apostles* 1:12-14; 2:1). Making a novena means to persevere in prayer and to never lose confidence.

A special 54 day Rosary Novena developed towards the end of the 19th century in Pompeii, Italy. It consists of the daily recitation of five decades of the rosary for twenty-seven days in petition and five decades for twenty-seven additional days in thanksgiving. In actuality, it is three nine-day novenas in petition, and three nine-day novenas in thanksgiving.

On the first day of the novena, the Joyful Mysteries are said, followed by the Sorrowful on the second, and the Glorious on the third. The Joyful Mysteries are then said on the fourth, etc.

The Luminous Mysteries or "Mysteries of Light" are said on the second day, followed by the Sorrowful on the third day, etc., by those who would like to observe them.

## Prayer Before a Rosary Novena

Holy Virgin Mary,
Mother of God and our Mother,
accept this Holy Rosary which I offer you
to show my love for you
and my firm confidence
in your powerful intercession.

I offer it as an act of faith in the mysteries
of the Incarnation and the Redemption,
as an act of thanksgiving to God
for all His love for me and all mankind,
as an act of atonement for the sins of the world,
especially my own,
and as an act of petition to God
through your intercession
for all the needs of God's people on earth,
but especially for this earnest request.

(Here mention your request.)

I beg you, dear Mother of God,
present my petition to Jesus, your Son.

I know that you want me to seek God's will
in my request.

If what I ask for should not be God's will,
pray that I may receive that
which will be of greater benefit for my soul.
I put all my confidence in you. Amen.

# III
# Indulgences
## *Indulgentiæ*

### WHAT ARE INDULGENCES?

According to the *Compendium of the Catechism of the Catholic Church*, "indulgences are the remission before God of the temporal punishment due to sins whose guilt has already been forgiven... Indulgences are granted through the ministry of the Church which, as the dispenser of the grace of redemption, distributes the treasury of the merits of Christ and the Saints".[1]

The Church teaches that "an indulgence is partial or plenary according as it removes either part or all of the temporal punishment due to sin"[2] and that "through indulgences the faithful can obtain the remission of temporal punishment resulting from sin for themselves and also for the souls in Purgatory".[3]

### INDULGENCES AND THE MARIAN ROSARY

According to the Church's *Manual of Indulgences*, "a *plenary indulgence* is granted to the faithful who (1) devoutly recite the Marian rosary in a church or oratory, or in a family, a religious community, or an association of the faithful, and in general when several of the faithful gather for some honest purpose;

---

[1] *Compendium of the Catechism of the Catholic Church* (2005), n. 312; cf. SAINT PAUL VI, apostolic constitution, *Indulgentiarum doctrina*, norm 1; cf. *Catechism of the Catholic Church*, Second Edition (1997), n. 1471.

[2] « Indulgentia est partialis vel plenaria prout a pœna temporali pro peccatis debita liberat ex parte aut ex toto » (SANCTUS PAULUS VI, Const. ap. *Indulgentiarum doctrina*, Normæ, 2: *AAS* 59 (1967) 21; *Catechismus Catholicæ Ecclesiæ* (1997), n. 1471).

[3] « Per indulgentias, fideles pro se ipsis et etiam pro animabus purgatorii remissionem obtinere possunt pœnarum temporalium, quæ consequentiæ sunt peccatorum » (*Catechismus Catholicæ Ecclesiæ* (1997), n. 1498).

(2) devoutly join in the recitation of the Rosary while it is being recited by the Supreme Pontiff and broadcast live by radio or television. In other circumstances, the indulgence will be *partial*".[1]

To obtain a plenary indulgence for reciting the Rosary, the *Manual of Indulgences* prescribes the following:

(a) The recitation of a third part of the Rosary is sufficient, but the five decades must be recited without interruption.

(b) Devout meditation on the mysteries is to be added to the vocal prayer.

(c) In its public recitation the mysteries must be announced in accord with approved local custom, but in its private recitation it is sufficient for the faithful simply to join meditation on the mysteries to the vocal prayer.[2]

Moreover, "to gain a plenary indulgence, in addition to excluding all attachment to sin, even venial sin, it is necessary to perform the indulgenced work and fulfill the following three conditions: sacramental

---

[1] « *Plenaria indulgentia* conceditur christifideli qui (1) Rosarium mariale pie recitaverit in ecclesia aut oratorio, vel in familia, in religiosa Communitate, in christifidelium consociatione et generatim cum plures ad aliquem honestum finem conveniunt; (2) eiusdem precis recitationi, dum a Summo Pontifice peragitur, et ope instrumenti televisifici vel radiophonici propagatur, sese pie univerit. In aliis rerum adiunctis vero indulgentia erit *partialis* » (PÆNITENTIARIA APOSTOLICA, *Enchiridion indulgentiarum* quarto editur (iulii 1999), concessio 17, §1).

[2] « Quoad indulgentiam plenariam pro recitatione Rosarii marialis hæc statuuntur: (a) sufficit recitatio tertiæ tantum eius partis; sed quinque decades continuo recitari debent; (b) orationi vocali addenda est pia mysteriorum meditatio; (c) in publica recitatione, mysteria enuntiari debent iuxta probatam loci consuetudinem; in privata vero recitatione, sufficit ut christifidelis orationi vocali adiungat meditationem mysteriorum » (IBID.).

confession, Eucharistic Communion, and prayer for the intention of the Sovereign Pontiff".[1]

> A single sacramental confession suffices for gaining several plenary indulgences; but Holy Communion must be received and prayer for the intention of the Holy Father must be recited for the gaining of each plenary indulgence.[2]

> The condition of praying for the intention of the Holy Father is fully satisfied by reciting one Our Father and one Hail Mary; nevertheless, one has the option of reciting any other prayer according to individual piety and devotion, if recited for this intention.[3]

> A plenary indulgence can be acquired only once in the course of a day; a partial indulgence can be acquired multiple times.[4]

---

[1] « Ad indulgentiam plenariam assequendam, præter omnimodam exclusionem affectus erga quodcumque peccatum etiam veniale, requiruntur exsecutio operis indulgentia ditati et adimpletio trium condicionum, quæ sunt: sacramentalis confessio, communio eucharistica et oratio ad mentem Summi Pontificis » (PÆNITENTIARIA APOSTOLICA, *Enchiridion indulgentiarum* quarto editur (iulii 1999), Normæ de indulgentiis, norma 20. §1; cf. aliæ concessiones, n. 5).

[2] « Unica sacramentali confessione plures indulgentiæ plenariæ acquiri possunt; unica vero communione eucharistica et unica oratione ad mentem Summi Pontificis una tantum indulgentia plenaria acquiritur » (IBID., norma 20. §2).

[3] « Condicio precandi ad mentem Summi Pontificis impletur, si recitantur ad eiusdem mentem semel Pater et Ave; data tamen facultate singulis fidelibus quamlibet aliam orationem recitandi iuxta uniuscuiusque pietatem et devotionem » (IBID., norma 20. §5).

[4] « Indulgentia plenaria semel tantum in die acquiri potest; partialis vero indulgentia pluries » (IBID., norma 18. §1).

*Appendices*

# Bibliography
## *Bibliographia*

*Breviarium Romanum*, editio typica 1961.

*Clementine Vulgate* (1592).

*Douay-Rheims*, American Edition (1899).

*Enchiridion Indulgentiarum: Normae et Concessiones*, quarto editur (1999).

*Manual of Indulgences: Norms and Grants* (U.S. Conference of Catholic Bishops, 2006).

*Missale Romanum*, editio typica 1962.

*Missale Romanum,* editio typica tertia 2002.

*Nova Vulgata: Bibliorum Sacrorum Editio* (1986).

*The New Saint Basil Hymnal* (Willis Music Company, 1958).

*The Raccolta: Prayers and Devotions Enriched with Indulgences* (Benziger Brothers Inc., 1957).

*The Revised Standard Version of the Bible: Catholic Edition* (Division of Christian Education of the National Council of the Churches of Christ in the United States of America, 1965, 1966).

*The Roman Breviary* (Benziger Brothers Inc., 1964).

*The Roman Missal*, Third Edition (U.S. Conference of Catholic Bishops, 2010).

# Index generalis

Præfatio   9

Prœmium   11

Rosarii Marialis recitatio   15

Orationes Rosarii   21

Mysteria Rosarii   41

Appendices

I.   Orationes variæ   92

II.   Novendiales   96

III.   Indulgentiæ   98

Bibliographia   101

**Domina Nostra Publishing**

P.O. Box 1464
Monterey, CA. 93942-1464
USA

info@DominaNostraPublishing.com
www.DominaNostraPublishing.com

CPSIA information can be obtained
at www.ICGtesting.com
Printed in the USA
LVHW071303310521
688948LV00023B/614